D0560510

think
BIG

Quotes, Notes, & Inspiration
to Spark Business Success

Bud Carter

simpletruths.com

Photo Credits
Cover image and internal images © weerapatkiatdumrong/GettyImages,
anon_tae/Shutterstock, graphixmania/Shutterstock, MSSA/Shutterstock.

Published by Simple Truths, an imprint of Sourcebooks, Inc.
P.O. Box 4410, Naperville, Illinois 60567-4410

(630) 961-3900

Fax: (630) 961-2168

www.sourcebooks.com

Printed and bound in the United States of America.
SB 10 9 8 7 6 5 4 3 2 1

CONTENTS

INTRODUCTION

F OR MORE THAN THIRTY YEARS, I'VE KEPT BUSY AT MEETINGS and conferences, jotting down the salient snippets shared by world-class speakers and entrepreneurs. My fascination with quotes started when I was an award-winning radio news editor, then a TV anchorman, and ultimately the editor-publisher of an issues and business weekly newspaper. I was recruited to become a part of an incredible business community called Vistage, eventually becoming their first chairman in the southeast.

Since my involvement with this international organization for company presidents and CEOs in 1987, I've heard more than one thousand world-class speaker presentations. Nearly one thousand opportunities to grab a sage bit of wisdom have presented themselves, resulting in a collection from the best and brightest minds across industries. Each quote has the potential to affect the way you think about your business, the way you innovate and excel. I hope you enjoy this latest collection and continue to grow every time you open its pages.

CHAPTER 1

PIT BULL MANAGEMENT

**Terse commentary providing laser-focused insight—
how no-nonsense, bottom line–driven management
behaves...or should.**

BY MOST STANDARDS, ENTREPRENEURS DRIVE OUR economy. The largest number of companies in our country are entrepreneurially owned, employing more than 70 percent of all workers, and have the most substantial bottom line.

As author Michael Gerber pointed out in his book, *The E-Myth*, most entrepreneurial companies are started by someone with an idea for a product or a service. Started by the only people who aren't guaranteed a paycheck when they put the key in the lock each morning. High risk, hopefully for a high reward.

Gerber goes on to note that most successful entrepreneurs ultimately recognize their company has outgrown them and that they need professional management if the company is to continue to grow and profit. Enter the professional manager, someone with a formal education specifically designed for this sort of opportunity.

The guy with the great idea probably still employs most of the people with whom he started, including those the company outgrew long ago. The founder generally wants to make sure long-term employees (now called *team members*) share in the success when the company is sold. And, if he fits the stereotype, the entrepreneur is a world-class champion at conflict avoidance. He has never fired anyone too soon, and many far too late. One CEO with whom I worked made the same report to his Vistage peer group each month saying, "I successfully avoided firing Scott for another month."

The professional manager likely has a guaranteed contract, providing him more money than the entrepreneur has been taking and maybe a shot at equity. He certainly has a detailed plan providing structure, process, and accountability. His job is to study the key indicators and make educated decisions based on the numbers and indisputable facts, but not on personal feelings or relationships. The professional manager subscribes to management coach Bob Thomson's mantra that the best thing you can do for a good employee is to fire a bad one. That, in a nutshell, is focused, tenacious Pit Bull Management.

In looking for people to hire, you look for three qualities: *integrity, intelligence, and energy*. And if they don't have the first, *the other two will kill you*.

—WARREN BUFFETT, CHAIRMAN AND CEO OF BERKSHIRE HATHAWAY

Don't cheat your people out of the **_opportunity to win_** because of your discomfort holding people accountable.

—MICHAEL CANIC, PRESIDENT OF BRIDGEWAY LEADERSHIP, VISTAGE SPEAKER

Most businesses rise or fall not because of the product, but the people.

—STEVE CASE, COFOUNDER OF AMERICA ONLINE (AOL)

<<<<<<<<<<<<<<<<<<<<<<<<<<<<<<<<<<<<<<<<<<<<<<<<<<<<<<<<<<<<<<<<<<<<<<<<<<

Never take advice from someone who doesn't have to live with the consequences.

—MARK CUBAN, OWNER OF THE DALLAS MAVERICKS

Conflict in most organizations is phony and designed to relieve people of having to take a risk and do anything significant.

—JERRY HARVEY, PHD, PROFESSOR AT GEORGE WASHINGTON UNIVERSITY, VISTAGE SPEAKER

Bad decisions made with good intentions are still bad decisions.

—JIM COLLINS, BUSINESS CONSULTANT, AUTHOR

....

As it turns out, plants and dollars can be managed, but people expect leadership.

—D. WAYNE CALLOWAY, CHAIRMAN AND CEO OF PEPSICO

Goals produce results,
not activities.

—JOHN MCNEIL, CHIEF CULTURE OFFICER OF CANCER
  TREATMENT CENTERS OF AMERICA, VISTAGE SPEAKER

The worst thing we can do is do
the wrong thing well.

—J. IRWIN MILLER, CHAIRMAN AND CEO
  OF THE CUMMINS CORPORATION

Never hire somebody who doesn't
raise the average.

—JIM KOCH, CHAIRMAN AND COFOUNDER OF BOSTON
  BEER COMPANY

If you haven't restructured your company in the past three years *you're in trouble*. A company is not a Catholic marriage—forever. *It's California style—one year at a time*.

—ICHAK ADIZES, PHD,
FOUNDER AND CEO OF ADIZES INSTITUTE

The most expensive time in a manager's life is the time between when *you truly lose faith in someone* and when *you do something about it*.

—JACK DALY, PROFESSIONAL SALES COACH, VISTAGE SPEAKER

We've got so many problems that we can't help but **solve** some.

—DAVID HANSON, FOUNDER AND CEO OF SYNCROFLO

....

Intolerable performance exists when intolerable performance is tolerated.

—DENNIS SNOW, CUSTOMER SERVICE CONSULTANT, VISTAGE SPEAKER

....

If your presence doesn't **make an impact,** your absence won't **make a difference.**

—UNKNOWN

You don't want to be in a commodity business unless you're the ***biggest, meanest kid on the block*** and you have the lowest price.

—JERRY GOLDRESS, CHAIRMAN EMERITUS
OF GGG PARTNERS, VISTAGE SPEAKER

If you can't change the people,
change the people.

—MICHAEL CANIC, PRESIDENT OF BRIDGEWAY
   LEADERSHIP, VISTAGE SPEAKER

If you don't make dust,
you eat it.

—BERNIE MARCUS, COFOUNDER AND CEO
   OF HOME DEPOT

Done is better than perfect.

—SHERYL SANDBERG, CHIEF OPERATING OFFICER
   OF FACEBOOK, AUTHOR

Everyone has a plan—
until he gets hit.

—MIKE TYSON, PROFESSIONAL BOXER

<<<<<<<<<<<<<<<<<<<<<<<<<<<<<<<<<<<<<<<<<<<<<<<<<<<<<<<<<<<<<<<<<<<<<<<<<<<

You can't build a reputation on what
you're **going** to do.

—HENRY FORD, FOUNDER OF FORD MOTOR COMPANY

<<<<<<<<<<<<<<<<<<<<<<<<<<<<<<<<<<<<<<<<<<<<<<<<<<<<<<<<<<<<<<<<<<<<<<<<<<<

Trust your gut; don't cover your butt.
They pay you to do what is right.

—PAUL RICHARDS, PROFESSIONAL BASEBALL PLAYER

Unhappy people attract other unhappy people, and in a small company that can *kill* you.

—CHARLIE KING, FOUNDER OF KING INDUSTRIAL REALTY

It doesn't make sense
to hire smart people and
then tell them what to do;
*we hire smart people
so they can tell us what
to do.*

—STEVE JOBS, COFOUNDER AND CEO OF APPLE

Only the paranoid survive.

—ANDY GROVE, COFOUNDER AND CEO
  OF INTEL CORPORATION

If you can't solve a problem, enlarge it.

—DWIGHT D. EISENHOWER, U.S. PRESIDENT

Every company eventually puts their
ox in a ditch. That's when you go after
their best people and customers, even
if your ox is in the same ditch.

—BUD MINGLEDORFF, OWNER AND CHAIRMAN
  OF MINGLEDORFF'S

Integrity matters.

—ANDY VABULAS, FOUNDER AND CEO OF I.B.I.S.

Recognize efforts;
reward results.

—CATHERINE MEEK, COMPENSATION EXPERT,
 VISTAGE SPEAKER

Excuses and results
are mutually exclusive.

—JIM BLEECH, CEO OF PARLIAMENT BUILDING PRODUCTS,
 VISTAGE SPEAKER

If you think all your customers are created equally, you're headed for bankruptcy.

—JIM CECIL, COFOUNDER AND PRESIDENT
OF NURTURE MARKETING, VISTAGE SPEAKER

The *telling difference*
between companies
in an industry is what
they do when things
go wrong.

—BUD MINGLEDORFF, OWNER AND CHAIRMAN
OF MINGLEDORFF'S

The reason marketing exists is to make it easier for sales to sell.

—JEFF FISHER, CHIEF SALES OFFICER OF I.B.I.S.

<<<<<<<<<<<<<<<<<<<<<<<<<<<<<<<<<<<<<<<<<<<<<<<<<<<<<<<<<<<<<<<<<<<<<<<<<<

Too many companies let bad leaders hide behind good numbers.

—RICHARD HADDEN, LEADERSHIP CONSULTANT, VISTAGE SPEAKER

Leadership is one of the things you cannot delegate. You either **exercise it** or you **abdicate it**.

—ROBERTO GOIZUETA, CHAIRMAN AND CEO OF THE COCA-COLA COMPANY

At the end of the day, you bet on people, not on strategies.

—LAWRENCE BOSSIDY, CEO OF ALLIEDSIGNAL

. . . .

The best way to keep a good employee is to fire a bad one.

—BOB THOMSON, MANAGEMENT COACH,
  VISTAGE SPEAKER

. . . .

When luck is your only backup strategy, it's really troubling.

—CLAY SHIRKY, ASSOCIATE PROFESSOR
  AT NEW YORK UNIVERSITY

You are not your target market.

—JIM CECIL, COFOUNDER AND PRESIDENT
OF NURTURE MARKETING, VISTAGE SPEAKER

It is not necessary to change.
Survival is not mandatory.

—W. EDWARDS DEMING, FOUNDER OF
THE W. EDWARDS DEMING INSTITUTE

Not harder, smarter.

—MATT STOUGHTON, PRESIDENT OF BLS ENTERPRISES

What kills a company is that stuff that is so quiet, so low profile, so off the screen, that you ***never see it***.

—DONALD PHIN, PRESIDENT OF HRSHERPAS, VISTAGE SPEAKER

If we want to maintain the quality, the integrity, and the whole culture of our company, *we've got to own it*.

"Why" is not a word used
by effective management.

—CHARLES LIPMAN, CEO OF DIVERSITECH

<<<<<<<<<<<<<<<<<<<<<<<<<<<<<<<<<<<<<<<<<<<<<<<<<<<<<<<<<<<<<<<<<<<<<<<<<<<<

Hire character. Train skill.

—PETER SCHUTZ, PRESIDENT AND CEO
   OF PORSCHE, VISTAGE SPEAKER

<<<<<<<<<<<<<<<<<<<<<<<<<<<<<<<<<<<<<<<<<<<<<<<<<<<<<<<<<<<<<<<<<<<<<<<<<<<<

Accountability requires
consequences. You can't
have one without the other.

—DON SCHMINCKE, PRESIDENT OF METHODS
   INTERNATIONAL, VISTAGE SPEAKER

27

The janitor gets to explain why something went wrong. Senior management does not.

—STEVE JOBS, COFOUNDER AND CEO OF APPLE

Good credit is for sissies.

—VINCENT FORESE, PRESIDENT AND CEO OF
  LINK-SYSTEMS INTERNATIONAL

. . . .

The second you get an inkling somebody is not working out, you're already late.

—JERRY GOLDRESS, CHAIRMAN EMERITUS OF GGG
  PARTNERS, VISTAGE SPEAKER

. . . .

The conditions necessary to cause your largest client to disappear are in place and have been activated.

—SAM BOWERS, CONSULTANT, VISTAGE SPEAKER

CHAPTER 2

YOU JUST DON'T UNDERSTAND

**Some things are obvious,
but only from the other side of the desk.**

DAVID WAS THE CEO OF A COMPANY THAT MANUFACtures pumping systems for high-rises and golf courses. As with most manufacturers, waste and "do over" work cost dollars that otherwise would have fallen to the bottom line. The guys on the floor just didn't understand.

It was end of the year, time for bonuses (a certificate for a Christmas turkey and a bonus tied to company profitability). Everyone—office staff, sales, engineering, manufacturing— gathered for their annual event, hands out, visions of big bucks dancing in their heads. Coming through the door, everyone spotted a couple of armed policemen standing on either end of a sheet draped table.

What was that all about?

David handed out the certificates and the bonus checks individually, with a word or two for everyone as he went down the line. Once done, he stepped back, and with some drama, pulled the sheet from the table, revealing stacks and stacks and stacks of money.

"That, what is on that table," he explained, "is how much money we wasted this year on scrap and having to do jobs a second time. That's money that could have been part of your bonus check."

With that, he started at one end pushing the all the stacks of money, under the watchful eye of the two policemen, into a trash can at the end of the table.

Before, they just didn't understand. Now they did.

Being a customer
is voluntary.

—CHARLES E. FOSTER, MANAGER OF
ALEXANDER LUMBER COMPANY

There's no such thing as a *sustainable advantage;* ask Kodak, Blockbuster, and BlackBerry.

—MICHAEL CANIC, PRESIDENT OF BRIDGEWAY LEADERSHIP, VISTAGE SPEAKER

All selling is about trust.

—DUANE LAKIN, PHD, MANAGER ASSESSMENT SPECIALIST,
  VISTAGE SPEAKER

~~~~~~

Winning alone is
a sorry celebration.

—ROB BELLMAR, EVP OF BUSINESS OPERATIONS
  OF WEST UNIFIED COMMUNICATIONS SERVICES

~~~~~~

Success unshared is failure.

—JOHN PAUL DEJORIA, COFOUNDER
  OF PAUL MITCHELL PRODUCTS

A reputation is easier kept
than recovered.

—RANDY FRETZ, CHIEF OF STAFF OF
  WELLS REAL ESTATE FUNDS

<<<<<<<<<<<<<<<<<<<<<<<<<<<<<<<<<<<<<<<<<<<<<<<<<<<<<<<<<<<<<<<<<<<<<<<<<

I am a leader; therefore, I must follow.

—UNKNOWN

<<<<<<<<<<<<<<<<<<<<<<<<<<<<<<<<<<<<<<<<<<<<<<<<<<<<<<<<<<<<<<<<<<<<<<<<<

If it is not in the interest of the public,
it is not in the interest of business.

—JOSEPH H. DEFREES, U.S. CONGRESSMAN

A relationship is not something that you pursue; it's what happens to you when you are *immersed in serving the dreams of your customer.*

—TOM PETERS, AUTHOR

When two men always agree, one of them is unnecessary.

—WILLIAM WRIGLEY JR., FOUNDER OF WRIGLEY

....

Communication is not a two-way street; nobody has to listen.

—BILL GRAHAM, COFOUNDER AND CEO OF FACILITY
   SOLUTIONS GROUP, VISTAGE SPEAKER

We see our customers as invited guests to a party, and we are the hosts. It's our job every day to make every important aspect of the customer experience a little bit better.

—JEFF BEZOS, FOUNDER AND CEO OF AMAZON.COM

Managers promote stability while leaders press for change, and only organizations that embrace both sides of that contradiction can thrive in turbulent times.

—JOHN KOTTER, HARVARD BUSINESS PROFESSOR, AUTHOR

It's hard to boss your buddies.

—LEO WELLS, CHAIRMAN OF WELLS REAL ESTATE FUNDS

<<<<<<<<<<<<<<<<<<<<<<<<<<<<<<<<<<<<<<<<<<<<<<<<<<<<<<<<<<<<<<<<<<<<<<<<<

The man who says he is willing to meet you halfway is usually a poor judge of distance.

—LAURENCE J. PETER, AUTHOR

<<<<<<<<<<<<<<<<<<<<<<<<<<<<<<<<<<<<<<<<<<<<<<<<<<<<<<<<<<<<<<<<<<<<<<<<<

Want to read your customer's mind? Too late. She just changed it.

—SAP.COM AD

A customer's desire to be ***treated with respect*** and have their ***business appreciated*** is the only "fixed" in the variable world of business.

—CLARK JOHNSON, CHAIRMAN AND CEO
OF PIER 1 IMPORTS, VISTAGE SPEAKER

Good customer service is not synonymous with masochism.

—MICHAEL HYATT, CHAIRMAN
AND CEO OF THOMAS NELSON PUBLISHERS

....

Never tell people how to do things. Tell them what to do, and they will surprise you with their ingenuity.

—GENERAL GEORGE PATTON, U.S. ARMY

....

People can't see it your way until you first *see it their way.*

—JACK KAINE, MANAGEMENT CONSULTANT,
VISTAGE SPEAKER

Most people don't need a boss; they need someone to listen to them.

—MAURICE MASCARENHAS, VISTAGE SPEAKER

....

If it's a really big deal, your salespeople will screw it up.

—TOM SEARCY, FOUNDER OF HUNT BIG SALES,
  VISTAGE SPEAKER

Your company's culture and your company's brand are really just two sides of the same coin. *Your culture is your brand.*

—TONY HSIEH, CEO OF ZAPPOS

You're not truly successful as a CEO until a client calls and you have no idea what he's talking about.

—WALT KISER, CEO OF LAW ENGINEERING

Consumers today are often better informed than the salesmen themselves.

—MARCUS SHERIDAN, CO-OWNER OF THE SALES LION, VISTAGE SPEAKER

Lower your price enough, and your better customers will leave you.

—CHUCK REAVES, SALES TRAINER, VISTAGE SPEAKER

Your customer will take
the word of a customer
service rep over that of
a salesman.

—CHUCK REAVES, SALES TRAINER, VISTAGE SPEAKER

....

People rarely buy what
they need. They buy
what they want.

—SETH GODIN, ENTREPRENEUR, MARKETER

If I say
something which
you understand fully
in this regard,
I probably made
a mistake.

—ALAN GREENSPAN, CHAIRMAN
OF THE U.S. FEDERAL RESERVE

We do not see things as
they are; we see things
as we are.

—ANONYMOUS

<<<<<<<<<<<<<<<<<<<<<<<<<<<<<<<<<<<<<<<<<<<<<<<<<<<<<<<<<<<<<<<<<<<<<<<<

Whenever you see a
successful business,
someone once made
a courageous decision.

—PETER DRUCKER, PROFESSOR AT CLAREMONT
  GRADUATE UNIVERSITY

A bonus is a gift.
People have no idea
how or why they got it.

—KENT ROMANOFF, MANAGEMENT CONSULTANT,
VISTAGE SPEAKER

Profit is the applause you get from *appreciative customers* and *committed employees.*

—KEN BLANCHARD, AUTHOR

When an idea is at
your desk, it's yours;
when it's up on the
wall, it's everybody's.

—TIM JONES, DIRECTOR OF STRATEGY OF 72ANDSUNNY

Agreement is a problem.
Once we agree with others,
we have to share their risk.

—JERRY HARVEY, PHD, PROFESSOR
  AT GEORGE WASHINGTON UNIVERSITY,
  VISTAGE SPEAKER

A great place
to work is one
where employees
trust the people they
work for, have pride
in what they do, and
enjoy the people they
work with.

—ROBERT LEVERING, COFOUNDER OF
THE GREAT PLACE TO WORK INSTITUTE

People are the only sustainable advantage of an organization.

—RICHARD TEERLINK, CHAIRMAN AND CEO
  OF HARLEY-DAVIDSON

....

You don't own your customers—you lease them, and sometimes for only a very short time.

—BERNIE MARCUS, COFOUNDER AND CEO
  OF HOME DEPOT

People remember people who remember them.

—MARSHALL FIELD, FOUNDER OF MARSHALL FIELD
  AND COMPANY

<<<<<<<<<<<<<<<<<<<<<<<<<<<<<<<<<<<<<<<<<<<<<<<<<<<<<<<<<<<<<<<<<<<<<<<<

Perpetual optimism is
a force multiplier.

—GENERAL COLIN POWELL, U.S. SECRETARY OF STATE

<<<<<<<<<<<<<<<<<<<<<<<<<<<<<<<<<<<<<<<<<<<<<<<<<<<<<<<<<<<<<<<<<<<<<<<<

The purpose of getting our folks
to join organizations is not to get
them to know everybody; it's to get
everybody to know them.

—CHARLIE KING, OWNER OF KING INDUSTRIAL REALTY

No executive has ever suffered because his subordinates were *strong and effective.*

—PETER DRUCKER, PROFESSOR
AT CLAREMONT GRADUATE UNIVERSITY

CHAPTER 3

THE UNFAIR ADVANTAGE

Every viable product or service has an "unfair advantage" over its competition. What's yours?

CHAD HAD BEEN RUNNING A START-UP COMPANY FOR several years. After doing well as a professional manager, he'd made the difficult transition from hired gun to entrepreneur. The company was all his—his and the bank's.

His Vistage advisory group had become concerned that as the company grew, it might be outgrowing some of its people. Chad was loyal—to a fault, his colleagues thought. The group had listened to a speaker who told them it wasn't a question of if, but of when a company outgrows its people. In Chad's case, the advisory group questioned his controller's continued employment.

Chad explained that his guy had been with him since day one. He had the numbers on Chad's desk each month within ten business days; he kept accurate financial records, reconciled the bank statements, and did a great job of making sure that not only were invoices being paid, but also that discounts were being taken.

"No longer enough. Should be getting more," group members challenged. "Consider making a larger investment (Chad saw it as overhead) and upgrade to a different controller."

Ultimately, with oft-stated misgivings, he did.

The lesson learned, quoting a source we've never been able to identify, was: "If your company were a ship, a good CFO would be in the bow charting the course, not on the stern recording the wake." Chad's top man in finance had done a great job of telling him what had happened, but had never considered moving to the front of the boat and looking at what was, or could be, next.

With a new occupant, the office next to the CEO's was soon providing a whole new palette of financial services. Trailing twelve-month charts took the seasonality out of the numbers. Lines of credit were more easily negotiated by someone who spoke bank talk. The new financial management guy managed cash flow, understood risk management, and likely most importantly, became integral to all the company's financial and strategic long-term planning. Upgrading his top man in finance proved to be an investment for which Chad was getting a great return. And an unfair advantage.

It's always good when followers believe in their leaders, but *it's even better when leaders believe in their followers.*

—MARDY GROTHE, PHD, PSYCHOLOGIST, AUTHOR, VISTAGE SPEAKER

Consider the postage stamp: its usefulness consists in the ability to stick to one thing *until it gets there.*

—JOSH BILLINGS, HUMORIST

Judge a man by his questions rather than his answers.

—VOLTAIRE, PHILOSOPHER

. . . .

Learning is the only sustainable source of competitive advantage.

—KARL HELLMAN, ASSOCIATE PROFESSOR
  AT PRINCIPIA COLLEGE, VISTAGE SPEAKER

. . . .

Leaders describe the future, compelling and with clarity.

—DAN BARNETT, OWNER AND CEO OF
  THE PRIMAVERA COMPANY, VISTAGE SPEAKER

Anyone who stops learning is old, whether at twenty or eighty. ***Anyone who keeps learning stays young.*** The greatest thing in life is to keep your mind young.

—HENRY FORD, FOUNDER OF FORD MOTOR COMPANY

Most people are much better at waiting to speak than listening.

—STEVE WILEY, PRESIDENT OF THE LINCOLN LEADERSHIP INSTITUTE, VISTAGE SPEAKER

Most people stay mediocre to protect against loss.

—MORRIE SHECHTMAN, CHAIRMAN OF FIFTH WAVE LEADERSHIP, VISTAGE SPEAKER

Discipline is the training that makes punishment unnecessary.

—ROBERT E. LEE, CONFEDERATE ARMY GENERAL

If you want to be **Superman,** you've got to learn to fly in bad weather.

—MICHAEL CANIC, PRESIDENT OF BRIDGEWAY
  LEADERSHIP, VISTAGE SPEAKER

<<<<<<<<<<<<<<<<<<<<<<<<<<<<<<<<<<<<<<<<<<<<<<<<<<<<<<<<<<<<<<<<<<<<<<<<<<<

Risk more than others think is safe. **Dream more** than others think is practical.

—ANONYMOUS

<<<<<<<<<<<<<<<<<<<<<<<<<<<<<<<<<<<<<<<<<<<<<<<<<<<<<<<<<<<<<<<<<<<<<<<<<<<

Culture is the **last remaining opportunity** to separate yourself in a commoditized world.

—DAVID FRIEDMAN, AUTHOR, VISTAGE SPEAKER

Good marketing makes the company look smart. Great marketing makes the customer feel smart.

—JOE CHERNOV, VP OF MARKETING OF INSIGHTSQUARED

Nothing gives one person so much advantage over another as to *remain cool and unruffled under all circumstances.*

—THOMAS JEFFERSON, U.S. PRESIDENT

The art and science of asking questions is the source of all knowledge.

—THOMAS BERGER, AUTHOR

You can't stop learning. You have to continue to change and adapt.

—JOI ITO, DIRECTOR OF MIT MEDIA LAB

If you can't make decisions and build relationships, you won't have a job in the future.

—MORRIE SHECHTMAN, CHAIRMAN OF FIFTH WAVE
LEADERSHIP, VISTAGE SPEAKER

In a time of drastic change, it is the learner who will inherit the future.

—ERIC HOFFER, PHILOSOPHER

....

The prize goes to the person who sees the future the quickest.

—WILLIAM STIRITZ, PRESIDENT OF
   WESTGATE EQUITY PARTNERS

....

An investment in knowledge pays the best interest.

—BENJAMIN FRANKLIN, FOUNDING FATHER

What we need is less process
and more passion.

—FRANK MAGUIRE, SENIOR VP OF KFC, VISTAGE SPEAKER

<<<<<<<<<<<<<<<<<<<<<<<<<<<<<<<<<<<<<<<<<<<<<<<<<<<<<<<<<<<<<<<<<<<<<<<<<<<<<<<<

Your attitude controls your
destiny—in business as well
as in health.

—JERRY KORNFIELD, MD, FAMILY PHYSICIAN,
  VISTAGE SPEAKER

<<<<<<<<<<<<<<<<<<<<<<<<<<<<<<<<<<<<<<<<<<<<<<<<<<<<<<<<<<<<<<<<<<<<<<<<<<<<<<<<

The definition of knowledge has
changed. Knowledge used to mean
knowing how to do something. Now
it means knowing where to go to get
something done.

—DICK GORELICK, PRESIDENT OF GORELICK
  & ASSOCIATES

The new source of power is not money in the hands of the few, but *information in the hands of many.*

—JOHN NAISBITT, AUTHOR

You'll never have all the information you need to make a decision. If you did, it would be a *foregone conclusion,* not a decision.

—UNKNOWN

It's more important to hire people with the right qualities than with the right experience.

—J. W. MARRIOTT, FOUNDER OF THE MARRIOTT CORPORATION

. . . .

Make sure that bad news travels quickly to those who can do something about it.

—MICHAEL LEBOEUF, AUTHOR

Commitment is essential in business. If you don't have it, you won't have any business.

—MICHAEL HYATT, CHAIRMAN AND
  CEO OF THOMAS NELSON PUBLISHERS

....

Skills and savvy get you to the top, but character's what keeps you there.

—RICK GOINGS, CHAIRMAN AND CEO
  OF TUPPERWARE BRANDS

In business the **_competition will bite you_** if you keep running; if you stand still, they will swallow you.

—WILLIAM S. KNUDSEN,
PRESIDENT OF GENERAL MOTORS

Every now and then,
a man's mind is
stretched by a new
idea or sensation,
and never shrinks
back to its former
dimensions.

—OLIVER WENDELL HOLMES SR., PHYSICIAN, POET

My first message is:
Listen; listen, listen to the
people who do the work.

—H. ROSS PEROT, FOUNDER OF ELECTRONIC DATA
  SYSTEMS AND PEROT SYSTEMS

Every time you fail, you get
a piece of the answer as to
how to succeed.

—DERRECK KAYONGO, CEO OF THE NATIONAL CENTER
  FOR CIVIL AND HUMAN RIGHTS, VISTAGE SPEAKER

The key is not
the will to win...
everybody has that.
It is the **will to
prepare to win
that is important.**

—BOBBY KNIGHT, COLLEGE BASKETBALL COACH

Under promise; over deliver.

—TOM PETERS, AUTHOR

....

The way to succeed is to double your failure rate.

—THOMAS WATSON, CHAIRMAN AND CEO OF IBM

....

Success is going from failure to failure without loss of enthusiasm.

—ANONYMOUS

CHAPTER 4

IN SEARCH OF THE MAGIC BULLET

**The tough answer is that there are no easy answers.
There are no magic bullets.**

MATT WORKED HIS WAY UP IN THE BUSINESS, ultimately buying out the current owners and attaching his manufacturing-distribution company to a rocket. His monthly report to his peer advisory group nearly always included an acquisition and increased sales. Focusing on Values (he capitalized the word), building a strong culture, and maintaining an unswerving commitment to quality, the company soon topped one hundred million, then two...and was on its way to three when the news came.

The new owner, the guy who took so much pride in the jobs he was creating, the markets he was opening, the changes he was effecting, was diagnosed with an illness that could only get worse. And stress had accelerated the deterioration of his health.

He'd been the target of others when the company was smaller. Now, in search of an exit that would let him retire to focus on his health and his rapidly growing art collection, Matt decided to take the company public. His plan was to turn the reins over to a professional manager, a new CEO. An IPO would open the door for his exit. That would be his magic bullet.

One problem: Matt was a very private guy who found it difficult to share the numbers. Each exec within the company knew how they were doing, but not the specifics of how the company was doing overall. Be that as it may, investment bankers put a book together, and Matt began what was planned to be a long series of road shows designed to whet the appetite for stock when the company went public.

Only it didn't.

Meeting with him at his office, I asked a question: "Matt, how are you going to handle monthly calls from a thirty-five-year-old analyst demanding to know why you're not providing unending quarters of ever-increasing profitability?" There was silence and then resignation that maybe his good idea really wasn't.

Matt made three calls, reaching Warren Buffett the third time. Buffett flew into town over the weekend and told Matt he "liked buying companies from owners who took pride and were enthusiastic about their companies." They shook hands on a Saturday and had the lawyers working on details Monday.

Matt's search for a magic bullet came to an end when he picked up the telephone on the corner of his desk and made three calls.

Simplify your message,
and repeat often.

—JOHN LILLY, PARTNER WITH GREYLOCK PARTNERS

....

The secret to creativity is the art
of hiding your sources.

—ANONYMOUS

....

Passion for who you are and
what you do will carry you
a lot further than just knowledge!

—BOB DABIC, VISTAGE GROUP CHAIRMAN

I believe that *you should praise people whenever you can;* it causes them to respond as a thirsty plant responds to water.

—MARY KAY ASH, FOUNDER OF MARY KAY COSMETICS

A comfort zone is a
beautiful place, but
nothing grows there.

—UNKNOWN

Patience, persistence,
and perspiration make
an unbeatable combination
for success.

—NAPOLEON HILL, AUTHOR

Leaders are
visionaries with
a poorly defined
view of failure.

—MICHAEL SIEGEL, ENTERTAINER

Being present has nothing to do with where your feet are.

—CHALMERS BROTHERS, MANAGEMENT CONSULTANT, AUTHOR, VISTAGE SPEAKER

....

We are drowning in information and starved for knowledge.

—JOHN NAISBITT, AUTHOR

I want to stay as close
to the edge as I can
without going over.
Out on the edge,
you see all kinds of
things you can't see
from the center.

—KURT VONNEGUT, AUTHOR

Almost all big mistakes
are made when people
*perceive things are
going well.*

—JASON BEANS, FOUNDER AND
CEO OF RISING MEDICAL SOLUTIONS

A certain amount of opposition is a great help; kites rise against, not with, the wind.

—JOHN NEAL, AUTHOR

''

A key driver for relationships, revenue and results, is simplicity.

—JEFF BLACKMAN, OWNER OF BLACKMAN & ASSOCIATES,
 VISTAGE SPEAKER

There is no such thing as
insufficient resources,
only insufficient resourcefulness.

—TONY HSIEH, CEO OF ZAPPOS

Ideas are a commodity.
Execution of them is not.

—MICHAEL DELL, FOUNDER AND CEO
OF DELL TECHNOLOGIES

Be a sponge. Curiosity is life.
Assumption is death. Look around.

—MARK PARKER, CHAIRMAN AND CEO OF NIKE

People invest in who you are and what you can do for them. One without the other only assures short-term success.

—JEFF BLACKMAN, OWNER OF BLACKMAN & ASSOCIATES, VISTAGE SPEAKER

A mistake happens only once; underperformance is a pattern.

—GREG BUSTIN, PRESIDENT OF BUSTIN & CO.,
  VISTAGE SPEAKER

<<<<<<<<<<<<<<<<<<<<<<<<<<<<<<<<<<<<<<<<<<<<<<<<<<<<<<<<<<<<<<<<<<<<<<<<

Transformation is never done; continuous evolution is critical.

—VICTOR LUIS, CEO OF COACH

Mere change is not growth. Growth is the synthesis of change and continuity, and *where there is no continuity, there is no growth.*

—C. S. LEWIS, AUTHOR

People in distress will sometimes **prefer a problem that is familiar** to a solution that is not.

—NEIL POSTMAN, PROFESSOR
AT NEW YORK UNIVERSITY, AUTHOR

Leadership is about taking the organization to a place it would not have otherwise gone without you, in a value-adding, measurable way.

—GEORGE M. C. FISHER, CHAIRMAN AND CEO
  OF MOTOROLA

<<<<<<<<<<<<<<<<<<<<<<<<<<<<<<<<<<<<<<<<<<<<<<<<<<<<<<<<<<<<<<<<<<<<<<<<<<<<<<

New? New is easy.
Right is hard.

—CRAIG FEDERIGHI, SENIOR VP OF SOFTWARE
  ENGINEERING OF APPLE

The best ideas for improving a job come from those who do it every day.

—JIM BLEECH, CEO OF PARLIAMENT BUILDING PRODUCTS, VISTAGE SPEAKER

The quality of your questions determines the quality of your life.

—LEE MILTEER, AUTHOR

If you're not having fun, there's no passion. If there's **no passion,** there can be **no success.**

—PETER SCHUTZ, PRESIDENT
AND CEO OF PORSCHE, VISTAGE SPEAKER

Eagles don't flock. You have to find them one at a time.

—H. ROSS PEROT, FOUNDER OF ELECTRONIC DATA
 SYSTEMS AND PEROT SYSTEMS

<<<<<<<<<<<<<<<<<<<<<<<<<<<<<<<<<<<<<<<<<<<<<<<<<<<<<<<<<<<<<<<<<<<<<<<<<<

Everything should be made as simple as possible and no simpler.

—UNKNOWN

If you have an opportunity to **_grow your company_** and you really believe in it, the capital will follow you.

—GORDON TUNSTALL, FOUNDER AND PRESIDENT
OF TUNSTALL CONSULTING, VISTAGE SPEAKER

The greatest difficulty lies not in persuading people to **accept** new ideas but in persuading them to **abandon** old ones.

—JOHN MAYNARD KEYNES, ECONOMIST

In times of rapid change, experience may be your own worst enemy.

—J. PAUL GETTY, FOUNDER OF THE GETTY OIL COMPANY

. . . .

Never have a strategic partner with values different from yours.

—JERRY GOLDRESS, CHAIRMAN EMERITUS
OF GGG PARTNERS, VISTAGE SPEAKER

Sometimes I think I understand everything—then I regain consciousness.

—RAY BRADBURY, AUTHOR

<<<<<<<<<<<<<<<<<<<<<<<<<<<<<<<<<<<<<<<<<<<<<<<<<<<<<<<<<<<<<<<<<<<<<<<<<<<

Sometimes the truth depends on a walk around the lake.

—WALLACE STEVENS, POET

Without vision, we have no context for feedback; we're just responding to what *someone else* values or wants.

—STEPHEN R. COVEY, AUTHOR

Your business success depends on focusing on *the things to come*— not the things that were.

—CARLOS RIZOWY, AUTHOR, VISTAGE SPEAKER

Spoon-feeding in the long run teaches us nothing but the shape of the spoon.

—E. M. FORSTER, AUTHOR

....

Every problem in business has already been solved.

—ROBERT STEPHENS, FOUNDER OF THE GEEK SQUAD

CHAPTER 5

HOW TO MAKE PENGUINS FLY

Brief Explanations of How to Accomplish the Seemingly Impossible

I F THE CONFLICT AVOIDERS OF THE WORLD HOSTED A competition, my money would have been on Mark. He had faith—blind, unyielding faith—that if he worked just a little longer, he could make his penguins fly.

They were a ragtag group of executives that Mark insisted were part of a team, and despite glaring issues, they performed that way—at least most of them did.

When the executives updated each other during Vistage peer advisory meetings, Mark was not shy about discussing the issues he was having with his manufacturing manager in Texas. The group finally pushed him into sharing the full details in executive session and then unanimously (a rarity in any room with sixteen CEOs) said he needed to fire Scott.

Mark explained that Scott had been with them for years. Perhaps if he had a little more time, maybe attended a few seminars, he would come around. Then started a ritual memorialized in anecdotal form.

For literally twelve months, Mark started each of his monthly updates with the same phrase: "I successfully avoided firing Scott for another month."

Poked and prodded by his contemporaries, Mark finally pulled the trigger and replaced Scott with an all-star—an eagle who, if you will, soared where there had only been a penguin that couldn't fly.

You can't make a good deal with a bad person.

—WARREN BUFFETT, CHAIRMAN AND CEO
   OF BERKSHIRE HATHAWAY

....

Bloom where you're planted.

—ANONYMOUS

Take people out of
the organization
the same way you
brought them in—
with respect.

—ANN RHOADES, VP OF HR OF WILMINGTON TRUST,
VISTAGE SPEAKER

Let your marginal employee work across the street.

—ERIC CORYELL, FOUNDER OF CORE CONNECTIONS,
  VISTAGE SPEAKER

An expert is one who knows more and more about less and less.

—NICHOLAS MURRAY BUTLER, PRESIDENT
  OF COLUMBIA UNIVERSITY

You miss 100 percent of the shots you don't take.

—WAYNE GRETZKY, PROFESSIONAL HOCKEY PLAYER, COACH

. . . .

Important and relevant are not the same thing.

—BRAD REMILLARD, FOUNDING PARTNER OF IMPACT HIRING SOLUTIONS, VISTAGE SPEAKER

Holding people
accountable
*who have no
sense of ownership*
is simply imposing
upon people.

—MARK AESCH, FOUNDER AND CEO OF TRANSPRO,
VISTAGE SPEAKER

Those having torches will pass them on to others.

—PLATO, PHILOSOPHER

———

The world makes way for the man who knows where he is going.

—RALPH WALDO EMERSON, POET

When you do things you have to do when you don't want to do them, the day will come when you can do the things you want to do when you want to do them.

—ZIG ZIGLAR, MOTIVATIONAL SPEAKER, AUTHOR

You have to **leave the safety of the sidewalk** to get to the other side of the street.

—DON COTTLE, MANAGEMENT CONSULTANT,
  VISTAGE GROUP CHAIRMAN

<<<<<<<<<<<<<<<<<<<<<<<<<<<<<<<<<<<<<<<<<<<<<<<<<<<<<<<<<<<<<<<<<<<<<<<<<<<

Really good employees **choose to do more** than "just enough."

—JAY FORTE, FOUNDER OF THE GREATNESS ZONE,
  VISTAGE SPEAKER

<<<<<<<<<<<<<<<<<<<<<<<<<<<<<<<<<<<<<<<<<<<<<<<<<<<<<<<<<<<<<<<<<<<<<<<<<<<

You take people **as far as they will go,** not as far as you would like them to go.

—JEANNETTE RANKIN, U.S. CONGRESSWOMAN

Culture follows
the leader.

—DAVID FRIEDMAN, AUTHOR, VISTAGE SPEAKER

You don't want to be considered *just the best* at what you do. You want to be known as *the only one* who does what you do.

—BILL GRAHAM, CONCERT PROMOTER

The new guy learns from the old guy who learned from the dead guy.

—SCOTT STRATMAN, CONSULTANT

....

Strategy is a commodity; implementation is an art.

—PETER DRUCKER, PROFESSOR AT
  CLAREMONT GRADUATE UNIVERSITY

You are far too smart
to be the only thing
standing in your way.

—JENNIFER FREEMAN, ACTRESS

Somebody has to do
something, and it's
incredibly pathetic that
it has to be us.

—JERRY GARCIA, SINGER/SONGWRITER,
THE GRATEFUL DEAD

Given a reasonable opportunity, *the people at the bottom* will make a disproportionate contribution to *the success of your company.*

—RICHARD PALMER, COFOUNDER OF TRIPLEJUMP, VISTAGE SPEAKER

People may doubt what you say, but they will believe what you do.

—LEWIS CASS, U.S. CABINET MEMBER

....

Nothing is impossible for the man who doesn't have to do it himself.

—A. H. WEILER, *NEW YORK TIMES* FILM CRITIC

If you listen carefully, *very carefully,* people will tell you where they're going, what they're willing to do. *Don't assume.*

—STEVE HARTY, PRESIDENT AND CEO
OF GREATER GREEN BAY YMCA

Success is not
determined by
flawless execution of
a plan. It is determined
by ***how people react***
to failure.

—DON SCHMINCKE, PRESIDENT OF METHODS INTERNATIONAL,
VISTAGE SPEAKER

See everything, overlook
a great deal, and correct
a little.

—POPE JOHN XXIII

<<<<<<<<<<<<<<<<<<<<<<<<<<<<<<<<<<<<<<<<<<<<<<<<<<<<<<<<<<<<<<<<<<<<<<<<

Results are ancient history;
how are you managing
the future?

—DAN BARNETT, OWNER AND CEO OF THE PRIMAVERA
  COMPANY, VISTAGE SPEAKER

If all possible objections must first be overcome, nothing significant will happen.

—SAMUEL JOHNSON, POET, WRITER

I had all the disadvantages required for success.

—LARRY ELLISON, COFOUNDER AND CEO OF ORACLE

Visibility is credibility.

—KAT COLE, GROUP PRESIDENT OF FOCUS BRANDS, COO OF CINNABON

Few things can help an individual more than to place responsibility on him and to *let him know that you trust him.*

—BOOKER T. WASHINGTON, EDUCATOR, AUTHOR

When you have a choice
to make and don't make it,
that, in itself, is a choice.

—WILLIAM JAMES, PHILOSOPHER

<<<<<<<<<<<<<<<<<<<<<<<<<<<<<<<<<<<<<<<<<<<<<<<<<<<<<<<<<<<<<<<<<<<<<<<

Management is about
coping with complexity.
Leadership is about coping
with change.

—JOHN KOTTER, HARVARD BUSINESS PROFESSOR,
  AUTHOR

The highest reward
for a person's toil is
**_not what they get
for it_** but what they
become by it.

—JOHN RUSKIN, ART CRITIC

If you only give people *what they already want,* someone else will give them what they *never dreamed possible.*

—UNKNOWN

Learn to say no and it will be of more use to you than to be able to read Latin.

—CHARLES HADDON SPURGEON, BAPTIST PREACHER

....

It's never too late to be what you might have been.

—UNKNOWN

Be careful how you spend your people.

—RICK DETIENNE, PRESIDENT OF LAMINATIONS

The only thing not replicable worldwide is your people.

—MORRIE SHECHTMAN, CHAIRMAN OF FIFTH WAVE
  LEADERSHIP, VISTAGE SPEAKER

Every single human **_becomes great_** when they set goals that inspire their heart and soul.

—ROXANNE EMMERICH, CEO
OF THE EMMERICH GROUP, AUTHOR

Faced with the choice between *changing one's mind* and *proving that there is no need to do so,* almost everybody gets busy on the proof.

—JOHN KENNETH GALBRAITH,
PROFESSOR AT HARVARD UNIVERSITY, AUTHOR

I much prefer people who **_rock the boat_** to people who jump out.

—ORSON WELLES, ACTOR, DIRECTOR, FILMMAKER

CHAPTER 6

SLIDING DOWN THE RAZOR BLADE OF LIFE

A key phrase from one of satirist Tom Lehrer's songs
evokes the pain of inevitable truths.

LYNN ANDERSON SOLD MILLIONS OF RECORDS REMIND-ing folks no one promises anyone a rose garden. Sometimes a made-for-each-other romance can end up on the rocks.

Walt had started as a professional manager in a financial services company and grew in rank and responsibility as the company expanded—until it hit a bad patch and rapidly plummeted to the point that bankruptcy was all but inevitable. Eager to avoid the stigma of having one of their companies go bankrupt, the folks at headquarters offered Walt the whole mess for a dollar. He agreed, with the provision that he also be given the money set aside to settle a spate of lawsuits.

The troops rallied, and Walt brought the company back from the brink. He was good at negotiating and started making money, profiting on the funds that had been set aside to settle pending litigation. Those funds were then used for hiring good talent and expanding services.

Life was good; Walt adapted to new technology and came up with a service that made it difficult for clients to leave. More and more black ink settled on the bottom line. Then the calls started. Was he, could he be, interested in selling? Having sold slices of ownership to his management team, he felt an obligation to listen, and as the numbers started coming in, it became obvious that he needed to sell if he was going to provide liquidity for the people who had worked with him to create this great success.

It came down to two companies: one was offering $49 a share, the other $53. The first was a company Walt knew well. They pledged to keep his team, offering him a contract, and had a culture that aligned closely with Walt's company's. The second was a by-the-numbers operation that thought people were largely expendable. They wanted Walt to stay through the transition, but that would be it. Their reputation was of having only one focus: the bottom line.

How much was enough? Walt told his Vistage advisory group that he was going to get a check for more than he ever could have imagined, and while he could then retire, his key execs likely would not, so he opted for less ($49 per share)—figuring that the money was more than enough and his goals of providing for his team and assuring their future were being met. And he'd stay on to help take the company to a new level.

Two years later, the company that finished second bought the company that finished first. Things changed, Walt's assumptions about that company proved correct, and he left. As satirist Tom Lehrer so graphically put it, Walt had taken "a slide down the razor blade of life."

That rose had thorns.

Partnerships are not made in the **womb.**

–BUD MINGLEDORFF, OWNER AND CHAIRMAN
OF MINGLEDORFF'S

....

One lifetime isn't enough. Just when you start to learn, **it's time to go.**

–LUIS MARDEN, *NATIONAL GEOGRAPHIC*
PHOTOGRAPHER AND WRITER

....

If you have everything **under control,** you're **not going fast enough.**

–MARIO ANDRETTI, RACE CAR DRIVER

Anyone not *pulling* his weight is probably pushing his luck.

—RANDY FRETZ, CHIEF OF STAFF
OF WELLS REAL ESTATE FUNDS

When things are bad,
we take comfort in the
thought that they could
always get worse. And
when they are, we find
hope in the thought
that things are so bad
they have to get better.

—MALCOLM FORBES, CHAIRMAN
AND PUBLISHER OF FORBES MAGAZINE

You just can't beat the person who won't give up.

—BABE RUTH, PRO BASEBALL PLAYER

<<<<<<<<<<<<<<<<<<<<<<<<<<<<<<<<<<<<<<<<<<<<<<<<<<<<<<<<<<<<<<<<<<<<<<<<

You can't make a good decision with bad information.

—KEVIN SCHMUGGEROW, REGIONAL MANAGER
  OF HEPACO

In God we trust;
all others must bring data.

—W. EDWARDS DEMING, FOUNDER OF
   THE W. EDWARDS DEMING INSTITUTE

The world's fastest
strategic planning session:
Where are you? Where
would you like to be? How
would you like to get there?

—JEFF BLACKMAN, OWNER OF BLACKMAN & ASSOCIATES,
   VISTAGE SPEAKER

Most companies grow themselves out of business; they either **can't finance it** or they **can't manage it.**

—DR. GERALD FAUST, FOUNDER OF COURSEWARE

If you choose not to decide, you have still made a choice.

—GEDDY LEE, SINGER/SONGWRITER, RUSH

The way we see the problem is the problem.

—STEPHEN R. COVEY, AUTHOR

You have to have
purpose, you have to
have **_vision,_** and most
importantly, you must
share it with **_the people_**
in your organization.

—DR. GERALD FAUST, FOUNDER OF COURSEWARE

Show me someone
who has done
**something
worthwhile,** and I'll
show you someone
who has ***overcome
adversity.***

—LOU HOLTZ, COLLEGE FOOTBALL COACH

There is more right with us than wrong with us, regardless how wrong we think we are.

—JON KABAT-ZINN, PHD, FOUNDER OF THE
STRESS REDUCTION CLINIC AT UNIVERSITY OF
MASSACHUSETTS

....

When it's over—no regrets.

—RANDALL PEETERS, PHD, AEROSPACE CHIEF SCIENTIST,
VISTAGE SPEAKER

If your horse dies, get off.

—SIGN IN KENTUCKY FIELD

‹‹‹

If you're not living on the edge,
you're taking up too much space.

—TOM FELTENSTEIN, SVP OF BOZELL ADVERTISING,
  VISTAGE SPEAKER

‹‹‹

Don't get so busy making a living
that you forget to make a life.

—DOLLY PARTON, SINGER/SONGWRITER

We must take change *by the hand,* or rest assuredly, change will take us *by the throat.*

—WINSTON CHURCHILL, PRIME MINISTER
OF GREAT BRITAIN

In a bullfight, the bull perceives the cape as the problem, but it is the sword that kills him. *Are you chasing the cape or the sword?*

—MIKE BELL, TECHNICAL SERVICES LEADER OF ADP,
VISTAGE GROUP CHAIRMAN

The truth will set you free,
but first it will piss you off.

—GLORIA STEINEM, FEMINIST, SOCIAL ACTIVIST

<<<<<<<<<<<<<<<<<<<<<<<<<<<<<<<<<<<<<<<<<<<<<<<<<<<<<<<<<<<<<<<<<<<<<<<<<

The only way I can tell
that a new idea is really
important is the feeling
of terror that seizes me.

—JAMES FRANCK, NOBEL PRIZE-WINNING PHYSICIST

You must have long-range goals to keep from being frustrated by short-term failures.

—CHARLES C. NOBLE, AUTHOR

We enjoy the comfort of opinion without the discomfort of thought.

—JOHN F. KENNEDY, U.S. PRESIDENT

The measure of success is not whether you have a tough problem to deal with but whether it is **the same problem you had last year.**

—JOHN FOSTER DULLES, U.S. SECRETARY OF STATE

Obstacles are those frightful things you see when you take your eyes off the goal.

—ANONYMOUS

....

No organization can make good decisions without conflict.

—IAN MACDOUGALL, FOUNDER OF CORPORATE
  LIFECYCLES, VISTAGE SPEAKER

....

A smart man knows how to grow a company; a brilliant man knows when to sell it.

—JEFF MCCART, CEO OF THE MCCART GROUP

Nobody *succeeds beyond his or her wildest expectations* unless he or she begins *with some wild expectations.*

—RALPH CHARELL, AUTHOR

Just think how happy you would be if you *lost* *everything* you have right now, and then *got it back again.*

—FRANCES RODMAN, AUTHOR

The longer it takes to close a deal, the less likely it is to happen; time kills deals.

—MARISA PENSA, CEO OF METHODS IN MOTION, VISTAGE SPEAKER

The fear of loss is twice the motivator as the desire for gain.

—DEAN MINUTO, SALES STRATEGY AND TRAINING COACH, VISTAGE SPEAKER

Even if I knew that *tomorrow the world would go to pieces,* I would still *plant my apple tree.*

—MARTIN LUTHER, PHILOSOPHER, THEOLOGIAN

Emotion in a negotiation is **tantamount** to giving a loaded pistol to a monkey.

—TOM PARKER, SENIOR VP OF YUKON,
  VISTAGE GROUP CHAIRMAN

. . . .

The man who views the world at **fifty** the same he did at **twenty** has wasted **thirty** years of his life.

—MOHAMMAD ALI, HEAVYWEIGHT CHAMPION BOXER

No one can guess the future loss of business from a dissatisfied customer.

—W. EDWARDS DEMING, FOUNDER OF
   THE W. EDWARDS DEMING INSTITUTE

Near-death experiences are very healthy for companies.

—DAVID COLE, CHAIRMAN OF
   THE CENTER FOR AUTOMOTIVE RESEARCH

I am convinced that if the rate of change inside an organization is less than the rate of change outside, the end is in sight.

—JACK WELCH, CHAIRMAN AND CEO
   OF GENERAL ELECTRIC

My interest is in the *future* because I am going to spend *the rest of my life* there.

—CHARLES F. KETTERING, INVENTOR, FOUNDER OF DELCO ELECTRONICS

Happiness comes from moving toward getting what you want, not from getting it.

—STEVEN SNYDER, FOUNDER OF SNYDER LEADERSHIP
  GROUP, VISTAGE SPEAKER

<<<<<<<<<<<<<<<<<<<<<<<<<<<<<<<<<<<<<<<<<<<<<<<<<<<<<<<<<<<<<<<<<<<<<<<<<<<<

Following the path of least resistance is what makes rivers and men crooked.

—UNKNOWN

<<<<<<<<<<<<<<<<<<<<<<<<<<<<<<<<<<<<<<<<<<<<<<<<<<<<<<<<<<<<<<<<<<<<<<<<<<<<

How come every time I get stabbed in the back, my fingerprints are on the knife?

—JERRY HARVEY, PHD, PROFESSOR AT GEORGE
  WASHINGTON UNIVERSITY, VISTAGE SPEAKER

If you are not careful, your *success in the past* will block your chances to *succeed in the future.*

—JOEL A. BARKER, AUTHOR, FILMMAKER

I don't care to be involved in the **crash landing** unless I can be *in on the takeoff.*

—HAROLD STASSEN, GOVERNOR OF MINNESOTA

If we don't change our direction, we're likely to end up where we're headed.

—CHINESE PROVERB

If there's no such thing as risk of loss, there is no potential for gain.

—LEO WELLS, CHAIRMAN OF WELLS REAL ESTATE FUNDS

Most see what is before them; the strategic leaders sense what is around the corner.

—KIRBY MARTZALL, FOUNDER AND CEO OF KL MARTZALL, VISTAGE GROUP CHAIRMAN

CHAPTER 7

SLAYING LIFE'S GOLIATHS

A few pebbles for your business's slingshot.

SOMETIMES THE LITTLE GUY WINS ONE. DAVID DID IT with a slingshot, and Jim did it with a set of keys. They both slew Goliath.

Years before, Jim had invested in and then later took over running a company in one of the most basic areas of manufacturing. But when the economy turned soft, business predictably slowed, and profitability was evasive. A much larger competitor had expressed interest in buying the company. A few weeks into the early talks, a new and very big problem surfaced. The Occupational Safety and Health Administration had found that the small plot of land Jim's company sat on was contaminated. That hadn't been a factor (or had slipped by due diligence) when Jim's group bought the company.

Remediation could cost a small fortune.

Making matters worse, the company was well into its five-million-dollar line of credit with the Big Bank Up North; the potential buyer appeared to be scared off by the OSHA findings; and with no profit from the company for the last quarter, the bank was calling its line. What to do?

The Vistage advisory group went from shades of dark gray to gloomy black. A peripheral player having problems making money in a declining industry now found itself sitting on contaminated land, with heartless bankers a thousand miles away wanting their money back.

Close the doors and take Chapter 11 bankruptcy was the consensus among Jim's peers. Then one wizened professional manager suggested that Jim "give it back to them. You don't have the money. It's over. Give the bank the keys."

Turns out they didn't want the keys. The bank decided that five million was a small price to pay compared to the unknown cost of soil remediation, never mind the likelihood of finding someone eager to buy.

The bank tore up the note, telling Jim to keep the keys and the company. David felled Goliath with a well-aimed rock and a slingshot; Jim won his battle by tossing the keys on the desk.

Seven-foot-one former basketball star Wilt Chamberlain may have put it best when he said, "Nobody roots for Goliath."

We live in an ***informational society,*** but information is ***not knowledge*** and knowledge is ***not wisdom.***

—KEN RUSCIO, EMERITUS PROFESSOR OF POLITICS
AT WASHINGTON AND LEE UNIVERSITY

The CEO's job
is to get 100%
out of everybody,
and everybody is
100% different.

—TIM RYAN, U.S. CHAIRMAN OF
PRICEWATERHOUSECOOPERS

The worst thing about fear is
the fear it's going to get worse.

—STEVEN SNYDER, FOUNDER OF SNYDER LEADERSHIP
GROUP, VISTAGE SPEAKER

<<<<<<<<<<<<<<<<<<<<<<<<<<<<<<<<<<<<<<<<<<<<<<<<<<<<<<<<<<<<<<<<<<<<<<<<<<<<

You can always see what goes wrong,
but you can't see the cause. Causes
are invisible.

—BILL SCHWARZ, AUTHOR, VISTAGE SPEAKER

<<<<<<<<<<<<<<<<<<<<<<<<<<<<<<<<<<<<<<<<<<<<<<<<<<<<<<<<<<<<<<<<<<<<<<<<<<<<

If you ain't first, you're last.

—RICKY BOBBY, CHARACTER IN THE FILM
TALLADEGA NIGHTS

People tend to *choose problems they cannot solve* rather than *make the choices or decisions they need to make.*

—LEE THAYER, COFOUNDER OF THE THAYER INSTITUTE, VISTAGE SPEAKER

You are either the leader
or you are led.

—CARLOS RIZOWY, AUTHOR, VISTAGE SPEAKER

What would you attempt to do
if you knew you could not fail?

—UNKNOWN

Unless you walk out into the
unknown, the odds of making
a profound difference in your life
are pretty low.

—TOM PETERS, AUTHOR

You have to do what you need to do before you can do what you want to do.

—HOLLY MIDDLETON, PHD, PSYCHOLOGIST, VISTAGE SPEAKER

"""

You have to have a dream so you can get up in the morning.

—BILLY WILDER, FILMMAKER

Values are like fingerprints—*nobody's are the same,* but you leave 'em all over *everything you do.*

—ELVIS PRESLEY, SINGER, ACTOR

Change in the marketplace *isn't something to fear;* it's an opportunity for you to *shuffle the deck.*

—JACK WELCH, CHAIRMAN AND CEO OF GENERAL ELECTRIC

We ask people to change without showing them what they can become.

—SHEILA SHEINBERG, FOUNDER OF THE CENTER
FOR LIFE CYCLE SCIENCES, VISTAGE SPEAKER

....

The wise man draws more advantage from his enemies than a fool from his friends.

—THOMAS FULLER, AUTHOR

You're not good at doing anything you only do once.

—SCOTT STEIDING, VP OF MORRISON HERSHFIELD

If the path were without risk, everyone would succeed.

—MICHAEL CANIC, PRESIDENT OF BRIDGEWAY
  LEADERSHIP, VISTAGE SPEAKER

The best way to resolve a problem in business is to address it before you're asked.

—MARCUS SHERIDAN, CO-OWNER OF THE SALES LION,
  VISTAGE SPEAKER

I've found that *luck is quite predictable.* If you want more luck, **take more chances.** Be more active. *Show up more often.*

—BRIAN TRACY, AUTHOR

There is only **one thing more painful than learning from experience,** and that is **not learning from experience.**

—ARCHIBALD MACLEISH, POET, AUTHOR

The company with the best
information wins all the time.

—PAT PRICE, EDITOR AND GAME DESIGNER

<<<<<<<<<<<<<<<<<<<<<<<<<<<<<<<<<<<<<<<<<<<<<<<<<<<<<<<<<<<<<<<<<<<<<<<<<<<<<<<

Regret and fear are twin thieves
who rob us of today.

—ROBERT J. HASTINGS, EDITOR, AUTHOR

<<<<<<<<<<<<<<<<<<<<<<<<<<<<<<<<<<<<<<<<<<<<<<<<<<<<<<<<<<<<<<<<<<<<<<<<<<<<<<<

You are not required to set
yourself on fire just to keep
other people warm.

—UNKNOWN

Life begins at the edge
of your comfort zone.

—NEALE DONALD WALSCH, AUTHOR

It is always your next move.

—NAPOLEON HILL, AUTHOR

If we did all the things we
are capable of doing, we would
literally astonish ourselves.

—THOMAS EDISON, INVENTOR

Power is *always dangerous.* Power *attracts the worst* and *corrupts the best.*

—EDWARD ABBEY, AUTHOR

The secret of a successful organization is to get ordinary people to do extraordinary things.

—PETER SCHUTZ, PRESIDENT AND CEO OF PORSCHE, VISTAGE SPEAKER

One must from time to time attempt things that are beyond one's capacity.

—PIERRE-AUGUSTE RENOIR, ARTIST

Man will **occasionally stumble** over the truth, but most of the time he will **pick himself up** and continue on.

—WINSTON CHURCHILL, PRIME MINISTER OF GREAT BRITAIN

There is **_no limit to what a man can do or where he can go_** if he **_doesn't mind who gets the credit._**

—MOTTO ON A PLAQUE ON RONALD REAGAN'S
WHITE HOUSE DESK

The trophies on one's shelf do not win tomorrow's game.

—BUCK RODGERS, VP OF MARKETING OF IBM

. . . .

Don't be afraid to fail, but when you do, fail fast and laugh at yourself.

—MICHAEL HOUSTON, CEO OF GREY NORTH AMERICA

Experience tells you what to do;
confidence allows you to do it.

—STAN SMITH, PROFESSIONAL TENNIS PLAYER

Everyone who got where he is
had to begin where he was.

—ROBERT LOUIS STEVENSON, POET, AUTHOR

If we can, why wouldn't we?

—UNKNOWN

It's a funny thing about life: ***If you refuse to accept anything but the best, you very often get it.***

—W. SOMERSET MAUGHAM, PLAYWRIGHT

If you do not develop a strategy *on your own,* you become part of *someone else's strategy.*

—ALVIN TOFFLER, AUTHOR

I've developed a new philosophy...
I only dread one day at a time.

—CHARLIE BROWN, CHARACTER IN *PEANUTS* COMIC

‹‹‹

If you're too busy to learn, you won't
be busy for very long.

—UNKNOWN

‹‹‹

The biggest mistake a man in
management can make is to back
down on a matter of principle.

—CLARENCE FRANCIS, CHAIRMAN OF GENERAL FOODS

Most people tiptoe
through life hoping they
make it safely to death.

—EARL NIGHTINGALE, RADIO PERSONALITY, AUTHOR

....

Once the game is over,
the king and the pawn
go back in the same box.

—UNKNOWN

People work *harder, longer, and better* if they believe their work is *meaningful and positive.*

—RICK RICHARD, CHAIRMAN
AND CEO OF COLUMBIA ENERGY GROUP

Revenue is the measure of how hard we worked; profit tells whether it was worth it.

—JOHN MCKENNEY, CEO OF MCKENNEY'S

There are few sorrows, however poignant, in which a good income is of no avail.

—LOGAN PIERSALL SMITH, AUTHOR

Life isn't about waiting
for the storm to pass.
It's about learning to
dance in the rain.

—UNKNOWN

<<<<<<<<<<<<<<<<<<<<<<<<<<<<<<<<<<<<<<<<<<<<<<<<<<<<<<<<<<<<<<<<<<<<<<<<<<<<

If you can see the path in
front of you laid out step by
step, then it's not your path.

—JOSEPH CAMPBELL, AUTHOR

CHAPTER 8

LET'S GET SERIOUS ABOUT HUMOR

Humor, appropriately applied in the workplace, can mean bigger deposits at the bank. Work should be fun.

To paraphrase, "THERE'S NO HAVING FUN IN BUSINESS." But of course there is, and done properly, there can also be a message.

Nationally known speaker-trainer Deanna Berg jested early in my career that perhaps a good motto for one of my CEOs would be "Wait for me. I'm your leader." His initial reaction was a faint smile. Upon second thought, he had realized that she'd given him a message.

As Mary Poppins said, "A spoonful of sugar helps the medicine go down."

Likewise, the West Virginia folk saying that "You can't get the water to clear up until you get the pigs out of the creek" has a humorous tone, but also a message for anyone reluctant to pull the plug on a staffer who just doesn't fit, maybe isn't pulling their weight, or doesn't align with the company's values.

Want things to be better, the water to be clear? Get pigs out of the water, the terrorists off the payroll.

Properly applied in the workplace, **humor can mean bigger deposits at the bank.**

Don't confuse being out of bed with being awake.

—JOHN O'LEARY, MOTIVATIONAL SPEAKER,
 VISTAGE SPEAKER

....

I don't know what we're going to do without you— but we're starting tomorrow.

—UNKNOWN

If you fall on your face, at least you're moving forward.

—RICHARD BRANSON, FOUNDER OF VIRGIN GROUP

You don't have to
be nice to people on
the way up if you're
not coming back down.

—COLONEL TOM PARKER, PERSONAL MANAGER
  OF ELVIS PRESLEY

You can fool some of
the people all of the time,
and that's enough to
make a profit.

—UNKNOWN

It always looks darkest just before it gets totally black.

—CHARLES SCHULZ, CARTOONIST
  AND CREATOR OF *PEANUTS*

. . . .

Work is the greatest thing in the world, so we should always save some of it for tomorrow.

—DON HEROLD, HUMORIST

Wherever I go, I have
to take myself—and
that spoils everything.

—MURRAY BANKS, PHD, PSYCHOLOGIST AND SPEAKER

When you are arguing with
a fool, make sure he is not
doing the same thing.

—UNKNOWN

You may not realize it
when it happens, but a
kick in the teeth may
be the *best thing in the
world* for you.

—WALT DISNEY, FOUNDER OF THE WALT DISNEY COMPANY
AND DISNEY WORLD

It doesn't matter *how many times you fail.* You only have to be *right once,* and then everyone can tell you that you are an *overnight success.*

—MARK CUBAN, OWNER OF THE DALLAS MAVERICKS

Thunder is good, thunder is impressive, but it's lightning that does the work.

—MARK TWAIN, AUTHOR

<<<<<<<<<<<<<<<<<<<<<<<<<<<<<<<<<<<<<<<<<<<<<<<<<<<<<<<<<<<<<<<<<<<<<<<<<<

Things are more like they are now than they have ever been.

—GERALD FORD, U.S. PRESIDENT

When the word *assistant* appears **twice** in your title, you can't really think you're a **senior official.**

—MICHAEL SHEPHERD, CEO OF BANCWEST

Orville Wright didn't have a pilot's license.

—RICHARD TAIT, FOUNDER OF CRANIUM AND GOLAZO

<<<<<<<<<<<<<<<<<<<<<<<<<<<<<<<<<<<<<<<<<<<<<<<<<<<<<<<<<<<<<<<<<<<<<<<<<

Nobody has to be perfect until you fall in love with them.

—DONALD PHIN, PRESIDENT OF HRSHERPAS,
  VISTAGE SPEAKER

Doing nothing is hard to do.
You never know when you
are finished.

—UNKNOWN

....

It's not a wake-up call
if you go back to sleep.

—GREG GUTFELD, TV PERSONALITY, AUTHOR

Whenever you've got **business trouble,** the best thing to do is to **get a lawyer.** Then you got **more trouble,** but **at least you got a lawyer.**

—CHICO MARX, COMEDIAN, ACTOR

People are living **longer than ever before,** a phenomenon undoubtedly made necessary by the **thirty-year mortgage.**

—DOUG LARSON, NEWSPAPER COLUMNIST

Ninety-five percent of people make up their own statistics.

—UNKNOWN

░░░

My opinions may have changed, but not the fact that I am right.

—ASHLEIGH BRILLIANT, CARTOONIST

Everything will be all right in the end. So, if it is not all right, **then it is not yet the end.**

—UNKNOWN

Money may not buy
happiness, but I'd rather cry
in a Jaguar than on a bus.

—FRANCOISE SAGAN, PLAYWRIGHT

Life is tough, but it's
tougher when you're stupid.

—JOHN WAYNE, ACTOR, FILMMAKER

There's no reason to be the richest man in the cemetery. You can't do any business from there.

—UNKNOWN

If I had any humility, I would be perfect.

—TED TURNER, FOUNDER OF CNN
AND TURNER BROADCASTING SYSTEM

There are three kinds of men. The one that *learns by reading.* The few who *learn by observation.* And the *rest of them have to pee on the electric fence for themselves.*

—WILL ROGERS, HUMORIST, ACTOR

People often tell
me that motivation
doesn't last, and I tell
them that ***bathing***
doesn't either. That's
why ***I recommend***
it daily.

—ZIG ZIGLAR, MOTIVATIONAL SPEAKER, AUTHOR

There are very few people
I trust in this world, and I'm
not one of them.

—RICHARD GRIMES, MANAGING DIRECTOR
OF GRIMES FINISHINGS LTD.

The way I see it, if you
want a rainbow, you
gotta put up with the rain.

—DOLLY PARTON, SINGER/SONGWRITER

The higher you climb the flagpole, the more people see your rear end.

—DON MEREDITH, PRO FOOTBALL PLAYER,
SPORTS COMMENTATOR

<<<<<<<<<<<<<<<<<<<<<<<<<<<<<<<<<<<<<<<<<<<<<<<<<<<<<<<<<<<<<<<<<<

The closest anyone ever comes to perfection is on a job application.

—UNKNOWN

Politicians and diapers have one thing in common: they should be **changed regularly** and for the **same reason.**

—UNKNOWN

I love mankind; it's people I can't stand.

—CHARLES SCHULZ, CARTOONIST
  AND CREATOR OF *PEANUTS*

....

Hard work never killed anybody, but why take a chance?

—CHARLIE MCCARTHY, EDGAR BERGEN'S
  VENTRILOQUIST'S DUMMY

The nine most terrifying words in the English language are "*I'm from the government* and *I'm here to help.*"

—RONALD REAGAN, U.S. PRESIDENT

A lot of fellows nowadays have a BA, MD, or PhD. Unfortunately, they don't have a *J.O.B.*

—ANTOINE "FATS" DOMINO, ENTERTAINER

If you obey all the rules,
you miss all the fun.

—KATHERINE HEPBURN, ACTRESS

If life were fair,
Elvis would be alive
and all the impersonators
would be dead.

—JOHNNY CARSON, HOST OF THE TONIGHT SHOW

A mission statement is defined as **"*a long, awkward sentence that demonstrates management's inability to think clearly.*"** All good companies have one.

—SCOTT ADAMS, CREATOR OF *DILBERT*

The trouble with quotes on the Internet is that it's difficult to determine whether or not they are genuine.

—ABRAHAM LINCOLN, U.S. PRESIDENT
(JUST KIDDING! AUTHOR UNKNOWN)

<<<<<<<<<<<<<<<<<<<<<<<<<<<<<<<<<<<<<<<<<<<<<<<<<<<<<<<<<<<<<<<<<<<<<<<<<<<<<<<<<

That's all, folks!

—PORKY PIG, LOONEY TUNES CARTOON CHARACTER

ABOUT THE
AUTHOR

BUD CARTER WON NATIONAL RECOGNITION AS A RADIO station news director in Kansas City before becoming a TV anchorman in Peoria, Illinois. There, he went on to manage a radio station and became editor-publisher of a political and business-oriented weekly newspaper. The paper won national news coverage for itself during the Nixon years. It was there that he borrowed Ben Franklin's concept of penny wisdom and featured a quotation relevant to the focus of the day on the front page of each issue.

He was recruited to become the first Vistage (then TEC, or The Executive Committee) group chairman in the Southeastern U.S. in 1986 and soon started noting salient snippets shared by the speakers appearing before his Atlanta-based groups. Promoted to help grow the organization in the Southeast, Carter "published" his first edition of a self-published work titled "Pithy Business Quotes" in 1989—so that new Vistage group chairmen would have business-oriented content for their members' meeting folders.

Since then, Carter and his groups have heard more than a thousand speaker presentations—and he has now published thirteen editions perpetuating the key points made in the speakers' pithy quotes. Bud has a couple degrees (Liberal Arts and Journalism) from the University of Missouri and serves on the *Reporter Newspaper's* board, as well as that of Vistage Florida and the Atlanta Braves 400 Fan Club, Major League Baseball's second largest. He previously served on the boards of Coles Business College at Kennesaw State University, publicly traded Columbia Property Trust, Wells REIT I, the Rockbridge Commercial Bank, DiversiTech Corporation, WaveBase 9, and Creative Storage Systems. For nine years, Carter handled TEC management responsibilities (in addition to chairing his own groups), and was responsible for TEC's growth in the Southeast.

Carter and his wife, Kay, reside in suburban Atlanta. Bud professes to five passions: baseball, the pursuit of the perfect barbecue, racquetball—a sport in which he strives to accomplish mediocrity, jazz, and the quest for still more pithy quotes.

Have a great business quote you'd like to share? Please send your favorite quote to Bud for his ever-growing collection! Submissions can be sent to budcarter@aol.com.